Date: 11/15/21

Brother and Sister

BY TORA STEPHENCHEL

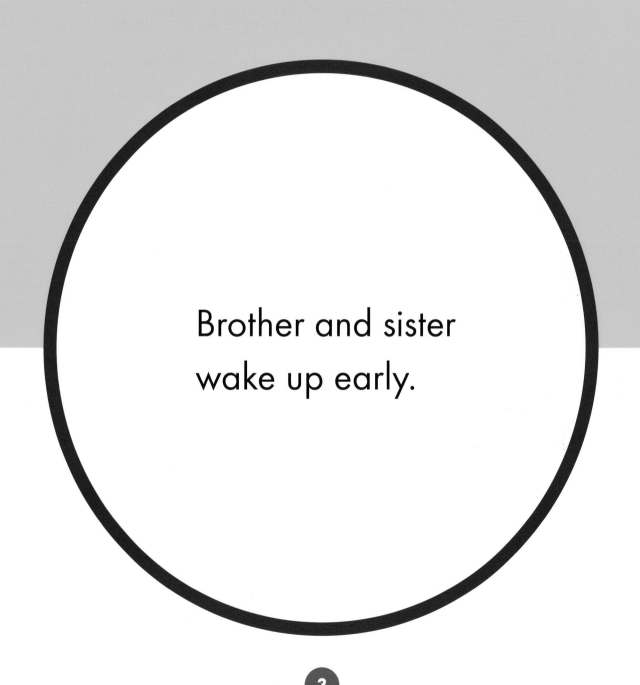

Brother and sister
wake up early.

Brother and sister
eat breakfast.

Brother and sister
read a book.

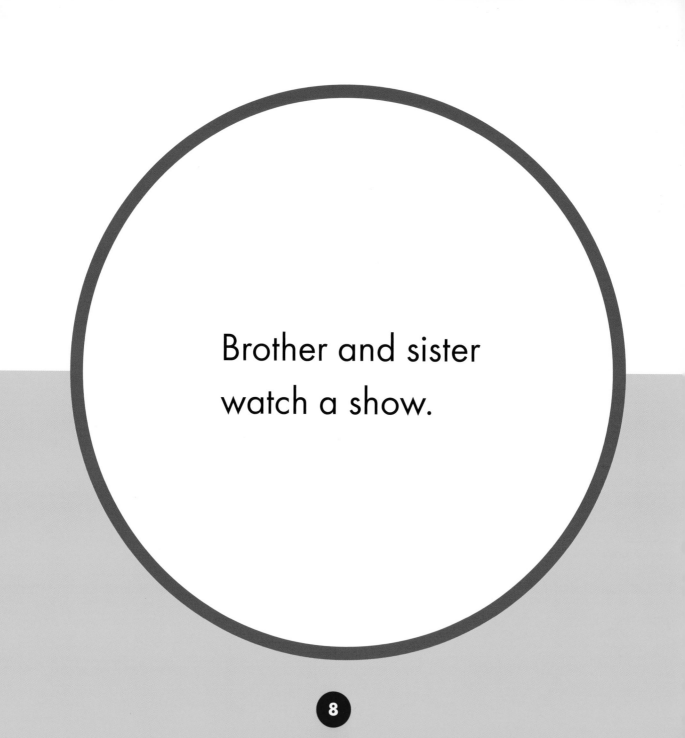

Brother and sister
watch a show.

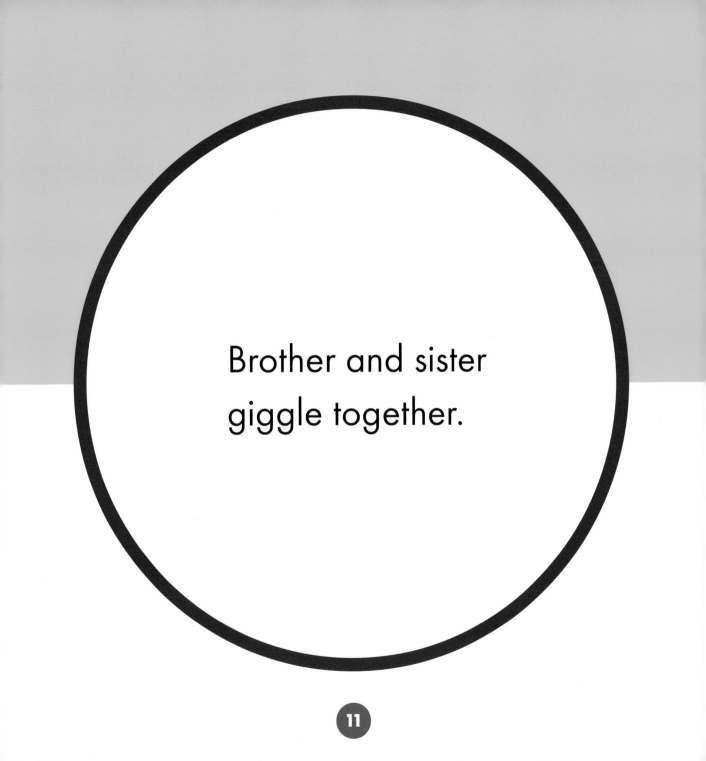

Brother and sister giggle together.

Brother and sister
go outside.

Brother and sister
fly kites.

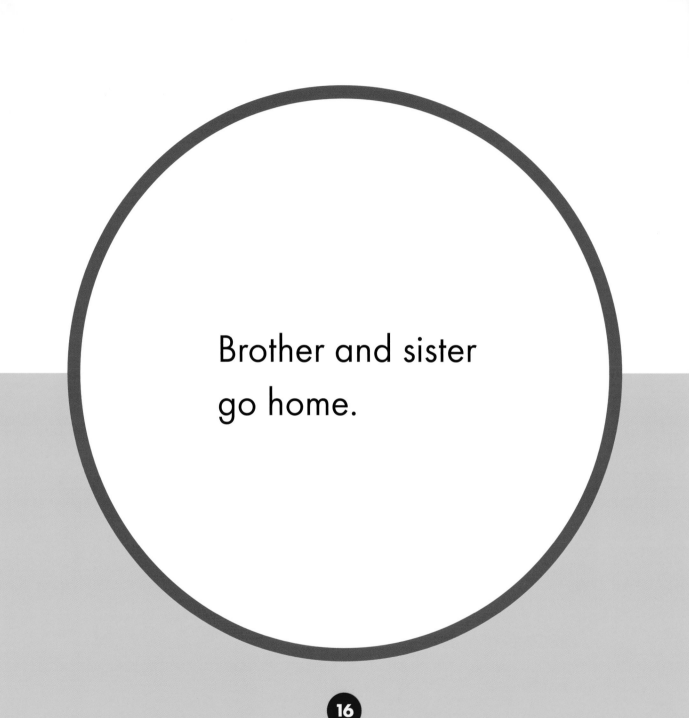

Brother and sister
go home.

Brother and sister
have a snack.

Brother and sister
had a fun day.

Sight words are a foundation for reading. It's important for young readers to have sight words memorized at a glance without breaking them down into individual letter sounds. Sight words are often phonetically irregular and can't be sounded out, so readers need to memorize them. Knowing sight words allows readers to focus on more difficult words in the text. The intent of this book is to repeat specific sight words as many times as possible throughout the story. Through repetition of the words, emerging readers will recognize, and ideally memorize, each sight word. Memorizing sight words can help improve readers' literacy skills.

and

brother

sister

About the Author

Tora Stephenchel lives in
Minnesota. She loves to spend
time with her son, daughter,
husband, and two silly dogs.

Published by The Child's World®
1980 Lookout Drive • Mankato, MN 56003-1705
800-599-READ • www.childsworld.com

Photographs © Anna_Pustynnikova/Shutterstock.com: 5; Imagenet /Shutterstock.com: 17;
spass/Shutterstock.com: cover, 1, 2, 6, 9, 10, 14, 18, 21; Tunatura/Shutterstock.com: 13;
Vitalinka/Shutterstock.com: 23

ISBN 9781503845084 (Reinforced Library Binding)
ISBN 9781503846517 (Portable Document Format)
ISBN 9781503847705 (Online Multi-user eBook)
LCCN 2020931110

Printed in the United States of America